Sneaker Hustle:
Making Money from Sneakers

LEONARD PAYNE

Copyright © 2019 Leonard Payne

All rights reserved.

ISBN: 9781702578677

DEDICATION

To my dear wife Lynne, who "puts up" with a lot and who hopefully, will be kept in the style to which she would like to become accustomed.

Thank You

I wanted to say a quick thank you for buying this book. As a way of giving you something, I want to invite you to FREE Sneaker Video Resources. Sign up here.

https://www.sneakercollecting.website/signup

CONTENTS

ACKNOWLEDGMENTS I

INTRODUCTION 1

1. SNEAKER TERMINOLOGY 5

2. THE BASIC METHOD 14

3. HOW MUCH MONEY WILL I NEED TO START 21

4. HOW CAN I BUILD MY INVENTORY? 27

5. HOW TO PRICE 32

6. SHIPPING AND OTHER COSTS 39

7. CAUTIONARY TALES 45

8. HOW ABOUT INSTAGRAM? 51

9. OUTRO 56

ACKNOWLEDGMENTS

For all those who helped and in some way may have contributed to this volume, thank you. You're helping to keep an old man in fine wine and cheese.

INTRODUCTION

A sneakerhead is defined in Wikipaedia as "a person who collects, trades, or admires sneakers as a hobby. A sneakerhead may also be highly experienced in distinguishing between real and replica sneakers. Sneaker collecting is a hobby often manifested by the use and collection of shoes made for particular sports, particularly basketball and skateboarding.
The birth of sneakerhead culture in the United States came in the 1980s and can be attributed to two major sources: basketball, specifically the emergence of Michael Jordan and his eponymous Air Jordan line of shoes released in 1985, and the growth of hip hop music. The boom of signature basketball shoes during this era provided the sheer variety necessary for a collecting subculture, while the hip-hop movement gave the sneakers their street credibility as status symbols. The sneakerhead culture has emerged in the United Kingdom and the Czech Republic in the last decade.

The cooler Urban Dictionary defines sneakerhead as

"One who is in love with but not limited to Jordans,

SNEAKER HUSTLE

Forces, Dunks, Maxes, etc.

Willing to camp out and face lines that wind around blocks for a pair of once in a lifetime exclusives!

On the verge of bankruptcy because the addiction is THAT serious.

Misunderstood by non sneaker heads as wasting money and are constantly told that they will get over it or that "it's just a phase.

Likely to kill you if you step on their kicks.

Running out of closet space because the boxes can only stack up so high...

Marks calendar for release dates and hates seeing fakes.

Lives for the first time they open the box and that new sneaker smell just fills up the air. HATES CREASES."

The fact of the matter is that its big business.

Sneaker market has grown by more than 40% since 2010 To an estimated $55 billion. In 2015 alone.
The athletic footwear industry in the US grew by 8%
Generating $17.2 billion in sales, with unit sales growing by 3% and the average selling price growing by 5%, to $102.00

Transparency Market Research said it expects the global footwear market to reach $220.2 billion in value and 10.974 million units by 2020.

The market for sneakers is booming, driven by millennial demand and a strategic business approach by the major players. According to SportsOneSource, the international sneaker market has grown by more than 40% since 2004, to an estimated $55 billion. In 2015 alone, the athletic footwear industry in the US grew by 8%, generating $17.2 billion in sales, with unit sales growing by 3% and the average selling price growing by 5%, to $61.15, according to The NPD Group. Among just the three major players— Nike, Adidas and Under Armour—sales increased to more than $25 billion in 2013, which represented a 47% jump from 2009, The Washington Post reported. Millennials in particular are driving this dramatic growth, spending $21 billion on footwear in 2014, a 6% increase from the year prior, with the biggest category being footwear over $100.

Nike's line of Jordan sneakers alone, which retail for around $100 to $200, boasted $2.6 billion in US sales in 2014, according to SportScanInfo. Sports shoes are "expected to have the largest market in terms of volume globally from 2014 to 2020," according to PR Newswire. Transparency Market Research said it expects the global footwear market to reach $220.2 billion in value and 10.974 million units by 2020.

So there's obviously Business. What we are going to talk about in this book, is the resale business in the words of a hip guy who is really into it. I use his words in his culture. Enjoy and Make Money

SNEAKER HUSTLE

1. SNEAKER TERMINOLOGY

Sadly, nobody likes a reseller for the most part, it is a hard job. It is a hustle. People will hate on you. But if you want

money, you want to hustle for money, there is a market to be made.

This is a one billion dollar industry. Resale is $1 billion of free money man, it's crazy. There's a lot for the taking. Don't think that Flight Club runs everything, Sole Supremacy runs everything. There is a lot for the individual reseller. With that, you got to walk before you can run guys.

We're going to go over sneaker terminology today. Sneaker terminology, what does that mean? We're going to be going over the terms that you will hear as a reseller and as a sneakerhead. Wait, what is that? What is a sneakerhead?

That's a sneaker term. **Sneakerhead,** It can be a lot of different things but for the most part it is people who are crazy about sneakers. They love their sneakers, they worship their sneakers, they put their sneakers in boxes like this and they just look at it. That's $300 and they just look at it. Crazy, crazy people. But they also have a lot of respect for the culture and like I said, sneakerhead is a loose term. It is a lot different now than it was back in the day. For the most part, it's always evolving so we got sneakerhead out of the way.

What is next? I say the word deadstock a lot. **Deadstock** or DS, what does that mean? A deadstock shoe is a shoe that has basically, it just got out of the factory. Bag is still attached to it, laces are still attached, laces are not laced up, shoe has never been tried on, still has that new leather smell for the most part, not used, deadstock. Deadstock shoe is a lot different than a used shoe. If you wear that shoe, it is not a deadstock shoe. If you tried on that shoe, it is not a deadstock shoe.

There are times where you may hear **VNDS**. VNDS stands for very near deadstock. Or, **PADS**, pass as deadstock. Both of these terms mean that maybe the guy cut off the lace bag, maybe they laced it up, maybe they tried it on in store. There's a little bit of dirt, little bit of stuff underneath the sole, but for the most part if you look at it and you could look at it quickly, it could be deadstock. That is the terms for that.

The complete opposite spectrum of deadstock, we got beaters. What are beaters? **Beaters** are destroyed shoes, shoes that you wear every single day and they are done. They have scuffs on them. They have marks on them, they have cuts on them, they have stains on them, they are beaters. later.

Much like a car, as I say, a "beater" in the sneaker world is a well-worn, likely older model of shoe that probably have some significant wear and tear on them. Beaters generally don't sell for much, unless they're a particularly legendary model, and they're generally sold without the original box or extra laces. Unlike most "worn" sneakers that have been kept as close to perfect as possible, beaters tend to be the shoes used for rainy days and in the gym. A "beater box" is exactly what it sounds like, it's a box full of beaters, and they can generally provide a good budget starting point if you're just looking to pick up some decent old kicks on the cheap.

Pro Tip: Know which shoes clean up nicely. Lower top sneakers with wider profiles like SB Dunk Lows, Air Jordan 3s, and most Nike Air Max models tend to hold their shape better over time than their higher and narrower brethren.

Another term you're going to hear a lot is resale. What is resale? **Resale** is the industry that we are trying to get everybody in this segment into. Resale is taking a shoe from a retail pricing and basically selling it for more than that retail pricing. I'm going to take $110 Jordan and if I can sell it for 150, that is a resold shoe and that is a profit of $40 and that's pretty cool. For the most part, most Jordans and most Yeezys have resale value, which means that once they are sold out you can't get them anymore. The value will go up over time and that is just simple business practise. It is called supply and demand. It is a very interesting concept, but for the most part, if there's a low supply, demand is high, the shoe will sell out, which means that the people that still want it need the pay a premium in order to get it. We'll go into that later on in a different chapter.

All right, another term you might be hearing a lot is **Colorway**. What does colorway mean If you know anything about fashion, design, or anything else visual, you're probably familiar with the term "colorway." It's just the color scheme for the given product. What's different for sneakers is that the colorway is often at least as important as the actual model of the sneaker. Are this year's "Chicago" Air Jordan 1s made of significantly better material than last year's "Black/Gum" colorway of the same model? Not really, but the colorway and slight rarity of the Chicagos make them worth roughly three pairs of the Black/Gum kicks on the open market.

Pro Tip: A colorway with a well-known nickname is almost definitely going to be worth more than one without, and that goes double for collaborations with other designers.

Next up we have **OG**. OG stands for original, meaning it's the first one of its kind. An OG shoe would be the 1985 Jordan 1 Bred. It never came out before. That's the first one, but they also have these things called retros.

Simply put, a **"Retro"** release is just a release (or re-release) of a colorway that happened after the shoe model's initial release, particularly in the Jordan Brand world. For instance, the original Air Jordan 7 dropped in 1992, but the Bordeaux colorway was re-released as a Retro (among many others) in both 2011 and just recently (2015). A new model of Air Jordan comes out each year, and while roughly half of them are generally unpopular with the public and therefore unlikely to be given the Retro treatment anytime soon, any of them could see a re-release whenever Nike and Jordan felt like it.

Pro Tip: Now that the Air Jordan line has been around for so long, the model that tends to be heavily retroed in a year is whichever shoe came out 23 (Michael Jordan's number during the prime of his career) years ago. Last year, the Air Jordan 6 (1991) saw several new colorways, this year it's the 7, and there are already releases planned for the end of the year and beginning of next year for more Air Jordan 8s (1993)

Next up we've got the word grail. **Grail** is you can think of it as like the holy grail. Your holy grail is something personal to you. It is a different shoe. It's usually a harder shoe to get, but a grail for the most part is something that means a lot to you. It's something that you're hunting after. For instance, my grail, the Jordan 4 Doernbecher, I really wanted this shoe. I wanted it in my size. I wanted it at a good price. My grail. Is it the hardest shoe to get? It is not, but for me that was really big time. It's not a Nike Air Mag, it's not the Eminem 4, but this was a grail and this is what I wanted, so that's pretty cool.

PP/Inv. Much to eBay's dismay, many sneaker buyers and resellers prefer to conduct business directly through PayPal since eBay takes roughly 10% of the final price. On social media, you'll see sellers openly state "$100 PP Inv" (meaning the sneakers cost $100 via PayPal invoice) or "$100 gifted" ($100 via PayPal friends/family). Since no one wants to get their eBay account suspended for using it as a platform to advertise PayPal deals, a lot of eBay sellers will simply put "Message me for a better price" or something along those lines instead.

Pro Tip: PayPal invoices provide a lot of protection for a buyer, but gifting payment or using Google Wallet generally doesn't. Unless you're positive the person you're buying from is legit, save yourself the hassle and only use the invoiced goods/services payments.

Yeezy. A nickname for Kanye West and any sneakers he's created or helped design. The first two models of Yeezys were made by Nike before the rapper recently switched to Adidas. It's pretty certain that anything remotely related to Yeezy will be significantly more expensive (and therefore have significantly more fakes made). The Nike Air Yeezy 2

"Red October" is still one of the most coveted pairs of kicks out there, but the Yeezy influence can be seen all across the sneaker universe.

Pro Tip: If you're going to buy any model of Yeezy, make sure you buy it from a legitimate store or reseller who's widely reputable. There are so many fakes out there, it's really not worth dropping a grand or more on something you're not absolutely sure is real.

GR/Limited. Regardless of how visually repulsive, uncomfortable, and/or impractical a sneaker is, if it's rare enough, people will still want it. "GR" stands for General Release, so they're usually kicks that'll be pretty easy to cop for right around retail. The more "Limited" a release is, the more expensive resale on it will be. It's basic supply and demand, although in this case, the limited supply drives the demand up as well. If you're looking to pick up some of the colorways brands make specifically for rappers, NBA athletes (Player Exclusive or PE models), and other celebrities, you better be prepared to shell out some serious money.

Pro Tip: Any special collection of sneakers, such as the annual Doernbecher Freestyle sneakers Nike makes in collaboration with kids at the Doernbecher Children's Hospital in Portland, are always going to be significantly more limited and expensive than most other shoes. If you want them, you'll either need serious money, connections, luck or automated sneaker-buying software.

Bred. The OG colorway of the OG Air Jordan, anything released in "Bred" (black and red) is going to sell out and sell quickly. Most models of Air Jordans (and other sneakers) worth their resale are available in a Bred colorway, in part because it's a well-documented fan favorite. If you want to start with a single colorway of kicks, Bred's a safe bet, particularly on an already solid sneaker silhouette.

Pro Tip: Almost any colorway with black as one of its primary colors is probably going to look good with a lot of different clothes, so aside from satisfying the hypebeasts of the world, Bred sneakers will probably match a lot of your closet.

Lastly, we have the term **Hypebeast**. What is a hypebeast? My goodness, I could literally write a whole chapter on this. A hypebeast is, I don't know, I don't know. A hypebeast is a different breed of animal. It's a different species of human being. It is a way of life. I don't know, man. It's honestly like some of the craziest stuff you'll ever see. Hypebeasts are people that literally drive the market. If they think a shoe is cool and they want to hype it up, they will get at it. They will buy it out. They will try to resell it and make it cool. Some examples of hypebeast stuff are Supreme. Supreme sells out no matter what. They make the weirdest stuff. They sold a brick last year for $200. It's ridiculous. That is a hypebeast.

But think of it this way, you are not a hypebeast. You are not a hypebeast by what you are wearing or what you're repping on your feet. There's a big difference because there's a lot of kids that will wear Yeezys and they're not hypebeasts. They will wear Supreme. They like the brand. They're not a hypebeast either. You are a hypebeast not by what you wear, but the attitude you have while you're wearing it. Your attitude towards wearing these kinds of clothes. If you're trying to stunt, I want to wear Supreme box logos because I want everybody to know I got money and I am the shit. That is a hypebeast man. If you're just wearing Supreme because you like skating and you knew Supreme back in the day, that is not a hypebeast. If you wear it casually because you think it's cool, that is not a hypebeast. If you try to stunt on everybody else and make everybody else feel inferior to you, that is pretty much a hypebeast man and you guys can contest it. But for the most part that's pretty true.

Become more and more of a derogatory term I feel like. But at the same time it's not a bad thing. Hype drives the market guys. Hype is kind of cool. At the same time, I would never spend 10 grand on that kind of stuff because that is crazy.
Lots of other terms

"A.C.G" – All Conditions Gear, a brand of sneakers produced by Nike
"B Grade" – shop-worn seconds sold at a discount
"Coke whites" – pristine white sneakers
"Crispy" – clean
"Cop" (used as a verb) – as in to purchase or acquire
"Cozy boy" – fashionable but also comfortable
"Deubre – also called lace tags are popular on shoes like Air Force Ones
"Dope" – fashionable
"Double up" – Buying two identical pairs of sneakers
"Drop" – Release of a new sneaker
"Feezy" – fake Yeezys
"Fire" – very good
"Fresh" – new and cool
"Fugazi" – fake
"Goat" – greatest of all time
"Garms" – clothes
"GR" – general release, or common
"Gum sole" – sneakers with solid rubber soles
"Gutties" – Scottish Slang term for trainers/ sneakers.
"Heat" – rare sneakers that draw looks
"High Top(s)" – a shoe that rises above or on the ankle mainly used for ankle support during sports.
"J's" – Another name for Jordan brand shoes
"JB" – the Jordan Brand logo (see below)

"Jumpman" – basketball player Michael Jordan, also can refer to the Jordan logo depicting Michael often seen on the shoes.

"Ice" – sneakers with transparent soles

"Instacop" – impulse buying

"Kicks" – shoes

"L" – loss/unable to purchase

"Lit up" – great

"Lows" – also called low tops are shoes that sit below the ankle

"Nib" – unworn, new in the box

"OG" – original, derived from the term "original gangster"

"Quickstrikes" – limited edition sneakers and prototypes with a regional early release, especially Nikes, and are highly desirable status symbols for American sneaker collectors.

"Reseller" – a person who buys large quantities of unworn popular sneakers to sell at a profit

"Red October" – all red sneakers

"Sitting" – referring to sneakers produced in large quantities that go unsold

"Steezy" – stylish

"Tonal" – Sneakers in a single color, as in monotone.

"Unauthorised" – counterfeit

"W" – win/successful purchase

"Wild" – amazing

SNEAKER HUSTLE

2. THE BASIC METHOD

There is a lot of basic information that we go over, there's more advanced information that we go over, but ultimately the goal is the same. If you guys are interested in starting to sell sneakers and trying to build up collections like this, by selling sneakers, then this is the videos that you guys want to watch. I know a lot of people are scared to talk about the topic of reselling. However, that is not the case for this channel, man. I built all of my sneaker stuff and this entire YouTube on the fact that I resell mystery boxes.

Now before we get into it, I do want to mention that this chapter is going to be a little bit more basic and I'm going to be going over the main basic concepts of how to sell sneakers. So, for some of you more advanced guys out there, I'm letting you know that this probably is not the chapter for you. However, there is a good amount of knowledge in here that maybe you guys can take away something from. So hopefully you guys stick around and read the material the whole way through. But this one will be tailored for the newer audience and the guys that really just want to start put their first step into the sneaker resale world. I think it's time we get into it, right?

Sneaker reselling changes every single year. What worked back in 2017 may not work here today, because the sneaker scene is different, there's going to be different apps you can sell on. There's different avenues to sell and just because markets flux all the time in terms of what is hype. With that being said, there is one big concept that we're going to be going over today. And a talking point that I hope you guys can drill into your heads when you guys are thinking about sneaker resale. And this is a common mistake that I see a lot of newer people selling sneakers always asking, they're usually saying things like, "I'm seeing that these shoes are super limited. There's like only a hundred pairs made, so the resale has to be crazy, right? I should definitely try to cop this one, right?" Hold tight there buddy, because you forgot another key concept of how to sell sneakers. Just because a shoe is limited doesn't mean it will resell.

The only factors that dictate higher resale value and the best potential profit that you guys can make is, one, low stock. However, you also need the second component which is high hype. Hype is important, guys. This is not about supply and demand which is a business concept at the commercial level of selling sneakers, it doesn't work on the aftermarket for selling sneakers, because it's not the same thing. I know a lot of people get confused by that wording but if you guys actually look at the definition and the business principle of supply and demand, it doesn't match up to what we're talking about. So cut that, it is not about supply and demand, it is all about supply and hype. Not supply and demand, supply and hype.

Again to reiterate, the optimal level that you guys want to reach for maximum resell potential, is low supply and high hype. When not a lot of shoe is being made, and there's a lot, a lot of hype generated around that shoe, that typically means that there will not be enough shoes to satisfy the consumer, and in those cases that's where people will spend extra money on top of the retail value, on the aftermarket so that they will be able to get that shoe.

Once a shoe is sold out, that's typically it. So that's literally the only option you guys have left because you won't ever have a chance to get that sneaker again unless they retro it, but you never know when that's going to happen and typically that happens years and years down the line. That's kind of a long time to wait and most people can't wait that long, so they're willing to pay an extra $300, $400 on top of retail in order to secure that pair now, while the hype is real. A shoe is only worth how much someone will pay for it, and trust me, people will pay for hype sneakers.

Now I'm going to bring up some examples right here of some current shoes that are trending right now. The current shoes that are trending now, and I'll show you guys how supply and hype affects markets right now, and currently in the year 2019 the world is run by Jordan 1 Travis Scott. It's been crazy this year for Jordan 1 Travis Scott and the hype is definitely real for that sneaker. Making it the perfect example of what we were looking for, high hype and low supply.

Now let's focus on the supply aspect. Most of the places like the news sources and stuff are saying that there is an estimated 20 to 40,000 pairs of Jordan 1 Travis Scotts made, which is not enough sneakers to satisfy the demand that was generated by these shoes. If you guys want to compare it to typical Yeezy drops, a typical Yeezy drop will have about 80 to 90,000 sneakers, and that is still always a sneaker that's sold out at 80 to 90,000 pairs, so you can imagine a 20 to 40,000 pairs it's even more limited, making it more coveted, making it more hype. So this will check off that low supply metric.

Next, we can talk about hype. The marketing hype was insane for the Jordan 1 Travis Scotts. I think Travis Scott actually previewed at some of his shows earlier in the year, and maybe even back in 2018. But people saw the shoe, and it's a Jordan 1 model, which is one of the best silhouettes you can use to resell sneakers. So it was a big deal, man. So what happens when that high hype meets low supply? That is right, money. These shoes retail for $160 and now they're going on the aftermarket for some at $1,800 plus. And this is in a span of two or three months, which is absurd. Like you guys don't see that kind of blow up in value ever. That's a very, very rare thing to see. $160 turn into $1,800, basically in a span of a couple of months, that's crazy.

And that is why high hype and low supply is important guys, because you can reach numbers like this when both of those factors meet up. Not bad for just selling one pair of shoes, right? That will pay some people's rent for a couple of months, dude. So, you guys can see the benefit of selling sneakers now. However, I want to let you guys know that that perfect storm of high hype and low supply is far and few between in the sneaker world, man. There's a lot of dud drops and there's a lot of different examples that we could go over in which it's a lot different than high hype and low supply.

So I'll give you guys another example of what high hype and high supply looks like and what kind of resell values you guys can expect from that. Now, another shoe that released in 2019, and a big one in terms of hype was the Jordan 4 Bred. This was a highly hyped shoe because this is like a shoe that was retroed back, I believe, eight years or so or something. It was a long time since the last pair released. Seven years, I think. It's highly touted as one of the classic Jordan 4 colour ways and it's just that Bred colour way, which everybody enjoys, no matter what Jordan it's on.

So a lot of people were thinking, "Well, there's a lot of hype over here. I can just cop Jordan 4 Bred and make a bunch of money, maybe make a hundred bucks off of it." Not so fast over there, man. We can take a look at our chart again. So the high hype is checked off, you guys know that Jordan 4 Bred is hyped, people want a pair of it. That's good. However, we also need to look at the supply factor. According to estimates, I was seeing that there was about 285,000 pairs of these Jordan 4 Breds on the market. We were just talking about the Jordan 1 Travis Scott, which had about 20 to 40,000 pairs, and I did have a quick mention that Yeezys were about 80 to 90,000 pairs. We're talking 285,000 pairs, guys. That is a bunch of sneakers on the market, that's a lot, a lot of shoes.

Even though the global demand still was over 285,000 and all of these shoes did sell out, there were still enough people that only copped a resell that were flooding the aftermarket. Those people were basically selling the shoes for about $240, where they retailed for $200. And when you guys factor in shipping and stuff, that would probably be about 220 after all is said and done. And then after fees, if you guys are selling on an app, like Goat app, that's another $20 or so. So basically your $240 sale turned into $0. Yeah, it's not always about hype. High hype alone will not sell sneakers.

Now we can get into the last example that I want to talk

about today, which is, the sneakers are very limited, there's low supply, however, there is also low hype. Now the Jordan 14 Supreme is a good example of this. It released, I believe, in two or three different colour ways on Supreme and some on Nike as well. And, I mean, it has Supreme in the name so you guys would assume that Supreme, it should have good resale value, right? Not so fast. Stock is always low for Supreme, so you guys already know that you can check off that metric, that there's a low supply. So hopefully there will be a lot of high resale value on these things. And the fact that you can only cop from Nike and Supreme makes it even more limited. So you would think that this is a good shoe to resell just because it's limited.

However, even though these were limited shoes, they didn't do anything in terms of resale. In fact, if you guys bought this shoe at a retail on release day, you probably lost money on it if you try to resell it on the aftermarket. "But they were limited. They were supposed to resell. What the heck happened? "

Good point. However you missed the key component where there was no hype behind it, man. So Jordan 14 model, which is typically not a very hype sneaker model in general, plus it just was very flamboyant and not very good looking at all. Not a lot of people were wanting it. I didn't see a lot of hype generated.

So in summation, supply and hype is everything, guys. I know it is a kind of basic concept, but I want you guys to be aware that just because there's low supply doesn't mean a shoe is going to sell. Just because there's high hype doesn't mean a shoe is going to sell. You need a factor of both of these things and to just be vigilant with the market and whatnot, which we will touch on in future episodes in order to make money selling sneakers.

And the second mantra I want you guys to have is to think always one shoe at a time. Low supply, high hype and also one shoe at a time. You guys don't need to buy in bulk in order to make money. Imagine if you copped just one Jordan 1 Travis Scott, you would have enough money to cover I don't even know, two or three beater boxes. So don't worry guys, you only need to focus on one shoe, you don't need a lot of money for that. 160 was what the retail price was, so even if you guys don't have a lot of funds, it's still possible.

SNEAKER HUSTLE

3. HOW MUCH MONEY WILL I NEED TO START

This chapter is going to be about how to become a reseller, how to do what I'm doing, how to make money selling shoes. Like I said, I make a good amount of money doing this, but it is not for everybody.

How much money do you need to start and how much money can you actually make from doing this reselling stuff?

I started off with $2,000. That $2,000 turned into, to date, in about eight months, 16,000, almost $17,000 and that's pure profit. That's not tax. That is straight cash. So, really cool. And I mean, like I said, it can be very, very profitable.

Do you need $2,000 to start? No, you definitely do not. How much money do you need to start, though, minimum? To answer that, it's kind of a little bit different because everybody's situation is going to be a little bit different. Some of you guys are like 14, 13, 15-years old, man. And then we got the OG guys that actually have real jobs and have cars and stuff and have money to spend. So, just try to hear me out.

We're going to go step by step. I want to try to hit all of you guys' viewership, not just one demographic.

So, let's start off with the young kids. Young kids from anywhere in middle school, high school, even elementary school, I guess, preschool, I don't know. There's preschool kicks. How much money do you guys need to start? Again, you guys probably don't have jobs. You guys probably get allowances maybe. If not even that, you guys save up your Christmas money. You guys save with your birthday money. Can you use that money to buy shoes? Yes, you can. What is the best way to go about doing that? So, let's say you have about $200. I think 200 is manageable.

Okay, let's make it 220. So, if you have $220, what you should be looking at is really, really cheap steals on eBay. And by cheap steals, I mean looking at auctions, finding shoes that are literally 30, 40 bucks and you know you can flip them for a lot more money. If you guys can't get ahold of that, the best way to double your money instantly is to save your money, wait for Yeezy release day, get on Adidas.com, try to cop a pair. And when you cop that pair, you can basically flip that automatically for at least 480 bucks, 500 bucks in which you just essentially doubled your cash.

Yeezys are a lot tougher to get than people think. It's not for everybody. And if you miss on release day, well, you know, it's okay. There's other outlets, like I said. Utilise eBay, utilise GOAT. Look for something a little that you know can sell high.

So, that's where the younger kids. For the older guys, if

you guys have like five, 600 bucks to a thousand bucks, that is a good amount of revenue. You can be like what I do. You can look at different outlets. So, for me, I look at the local outlet first. A lot of local sales will definitely be cheaper than GOAT, StockX, eBay. So, check your local sneaker forums. There's a lot of groups on Facebook. If you're in Atlanta, I know there's an Atlanta Facebook page. California probably has multiple, multiple Facebook pages. Hawaii has Hawaii sneaker heads.

So, with that, take a look in those forums, find the cheap steals and flip those shoes. Okay? You don't need a lot of money to start ramping up your business, okay? Like I said, start off with one pair. Don't go crazy, okay? The worst thing you can do is buy a whole mess of stuff at your nearest Foot Locker thinking it's going to flip. Not every shoe flips, guys. Not every shoe can flip. So, really start paying attention. Do your research. How much money do you have and what is a reasonable amount to spend? I do not want you guys spending all of your allowance, your savings, things like that on shoes because it doesn't sell instantly.

What you're going to do is you're going to turn this $200 that you were saving and it's going to turn into this. See, it's going to turn into a shoe and you can't spend a shoe, man.

A shoe is only as valuable as what you can flip it for. If you want to wear it, that's super chill. I mean, wear your kicks. That's dope. But this entire book is on reselling. So, a shoe itself cannot be seen as money, okay? Think of it as just a shoe. It is $0 until you resell it for actual money, okay? So, you might sit on that shoe for a really, really long time. So, be prepared. Have money in the back. Have money in your savings so you do not get stuck with zero income and you only have a shoe that you can't use until you resell.

So, how much money can you actually make? That's the next big question. So, you know you have to start off with at least a couple hundred. I'm sorry. Doing it with like 20 bucks isn't going to work. Shoes nowadays, even at retail, they're at least a hundred bucks. So, start off slow. If you can make up any profit of about $40 on a shoe, $40 is a good profit, okay? So, say you pick up... You find a good pair of alternate Motorsports or whatever it's called. If you find a good pair of Motorsport 4s and it's on sale, like you find it at like an outlet or something and it's like a hundred bucks, Motorsport 4s can typically sell for about $140. So, what does that mean? You just turned that hundred dollar Motorsport 4 that you found on sale, sold it to somebody else for 140 and you just pocketed $40.

Awesome. You just made like 40 bucks. That hundred just turned into 140. So, you now have 140 to spend in revenue rather than just a hundred and you just keep quantifying that, guys. You keep building on that. For me, I never stopped utilising my profits. So, I'm spending all of that 16,000 all the time. You guys wonder how do I buy all those 2,000 dollar boxes like every week? That's how. I don't see that as anything other than more revenue to build up on this. And like I said, it works, okay? This isn't some get rich quick scheme. This isn't some Ponzi scheme. This isn't a pyramid scheme. This is like a literal hustle. It's not going to be easy, takes a long time. Like I said, don't sit on these things for a long time.

People before would think, "Okay, I'm going to buy a pair of Jordan 1s, wait like a couple of months. It's going to be worth big money." It's not like that anymore, guys. It's all about volume and moving shoes quickly because the market is so in flux right now. It's not safe. So, you don't want to hold onto a bunch of shoes that are just going to become bricks, AKA Yeezy Calabasas, AKA the

Waverunner 700s. You can't predict the market for the most part. It's really tough. So, try to move the shoes as fast as you can, volume-wise, and just really find the competitive market pricing.

So, clear cut answer again, let's go over what we just learned. If you're a young kid, 200 bucks is a good place to start. Find one shoe at a time. If you are in college and you have a good part-time job and you have a couple extra bucks lying around, don't know how to dabble in the stock market yet and you want to try to invest it, buy a couple of shoes. Buy like two or three and try to flip it from there. You're going to turn it into $20 profit, $30 profit, $60 profit. All of that comes back, reinvest it again. What's amazing and really cool about shoes is that you can buy it and it will never be $0. A shoe will never be $0. I've sold literally the craziest ugly shoes and it makes at least a couple of bucks back and that's ridiculous. So, everything has value. Okay?

Again, if you guys are a young kid and you're just starting off, you have a couple of your old shoes lying around, start with that. You don't even need to spend any money. You can get rid of that old LeBron that you used to ball out in and you outgrew. That'll be your starting source of revenue, man. That'll be awesome. So, start with that. Start small, but think big, okay? Don't be satisfied with your $20 flip, with your $30 flip. Think bigger. We're not thinking in a Greek kind of way. We're not doing a bot system, like I said, but we're grinding. This is a hustle.

Making a sale is really cool and it teaches you a lot of good business practises, to be honest. So, start your grind, save money, but make sure you're not investing every single penny you have into this because it does take a good amount of time to start up. The benefits, man, they speak for themselves. You can make some crazy profit margins.

There's a lot of different things we're going to cover. Like I said, where to sell, where to buy, specifically. I told you guys a couple, eBay and GOAT, stuff like that but we can go way more in-depth on this stuff. It is not one-dimensional. This is a multidimensional thing.

Start thinking, start saving, start planning, start educating yourself on the market, and its fun. Have fun with it, man. These are shoes. You'll have a lot of fun doing this. You'll learn a lot, you'll learn the history of shoes, you'll learn how to interact with people and it's just really nice, man.

SNEAKER HUSTLE

4. HOW CAN I BUILD MY INVENTORY?

Inventory can come from a lot of different places like I've said. If you guys are just starting out, depending on what your age group is or what demographic you are, it's going to be a little bit harder if you're younger to kind of get to these avenues and we'll kind of go in depth later why.

But first off, the best, best, best resource you can be using is to look at the GOAT app. So GOAT app is how I find all my pricing on shoes and stuff. But GOAT app is really, really legit. What I like about it is that you know for sure your shoes are 100% authentic and in the sneaker industry man, or the sneaker resale game, if you sell one pair of unauthentic shoes, your credibility goes right down the drain. So that's why I only sell shoes from Sole Supremacy because I know that they legit check it well in advance. I buy shoes from GOAT because I know the same thing. It's 100% authentic.

So that's one of the nice caveats of having that GOAT app experience. For the most part, what you're going to try to do is you're going to look at that homepage and that homepage, I think, it doesn't specifically say it, but I'm pretty sure it uploads the newest items that have just uploaded onto the store. So you'll see the recent posts, the recent shoes that people are trying to sell. Look for the ones that are obviously a little bit lower than what you want, that way you have some room to flip. For the most part you'll see only competitive market pricing, but there will be a few shoes where it's severely undervalued and that's the one where you jump on, take it, let it get authenticated, come to you, and then re-flip it.

So that's one avenue, GOAT app. It's usually the best thing that I do . You get a card with your shoes that signifies that it went to GOAT and that's how you know it's not a fake pair. There's a lot of fakes running around guys. You guys got to be really secure and know where you're purchasing from. So I found some cream Ultraboosts, like I said, looking for deals online. Cream Ultraboost, if you guys don't know, typically go for about 500 something dollars. These I got for 270. $270 guys. That's crazy. So that right there, that means that I can flip this for 200 something dollars. That's ridiculous. The fact that it's in my size makes it so much better because if I want to keep it, I'm just going to keep it. Awesome. That's one avenue you can use though, GOAT app.

And the other avenue would be StockX. I'm not a big advocate for StockX just because the only things you can buy and sell on Stock are DS or deadstock shoes. The problem with that is that deadstock shoes will always be in that same competitive market pricing, so there's not really much room to flip. If you can't get a shoe for retail, then there's not really a point of trying to buy something on StockX and then flipping it on StockX. There is just not a lot of room for growth there. Fees are crazy, we'll get into that later, but yeah, StockX is an avenue, not the best, but you might find some good deals on there to buy shoes.

The next one, eBay. I used to use eBay all the time when I first started out. The reason being is because eBay has an auction format. So with auction bidding for shoes, you can get shoes for really, really cheap. So the best way for me to show you guys or tell you guys how to do this is to search ... Okay, for me, I search Jordans, so you type in Jordans, you switch the parameters or the settings to auction format, and then you go to ending soonest, so that way what you're going to do is do a thing we call it eBay sniping. So you watch that ticker, the timer going down, down, down, and when there's about like five seconds left, you put in a bid. That way you get the shoe for the lowest price possible. And that way you have the most opportunity to flip it for higher value.

So you just got to really look. Make sure you give yourself enough time when you're looking at this ending soonest though, so that you can make sure the pictures are legit, the seller is legit, and you know what the price is. Do not overbid for shoes. For example, those cream Ultraboost. If I bought them for 540 on eBay, there's no room for a flip because that's above competitive market pricing so I just mess myself up. So unless it's a big steal, don't do it. eBay can be sketchy, like I said, there's no authentication GOAT app card, there's no StockX authentication tag, so you really got to be careful. Only buy from people that have reputable selling reputation, so 100% feedback, and make sure that those pictures are legit checked. That's the best thing I can tell you there. If they have less than 10 transactions, I never buy from them. Even less than 50 sometimes I get a little bit sketched out. So just be careful.

So the last avenue that we're going to talk about is buying and selling locally. This way you can build up your inventory as well. Buying locally can actually be the best way to find cheap shoes because local meetups, there's no taxes, there's no fees, there's no shipping costs. It's just a straight up transaction, shoe for cash. Again, it does have its flaws. So while you're going to get shoes for really cheap, you again do not know if it's authentic or not. You got to really make sure that you can find tagged pictures. Tagged pictures would be putting your ID or somebody put something next to that picture so it's not a stock photo from the internet. That way, you know when you get the item it's like, okay, that's their item. It's not something that they just showed on, you know, from Google.

So that's one way to check. Make sure that the forum that you're in is moderated and everything is legit. Go to your local Facebook forum, find the page that sells sneakers in wherever you're living and try to buy locally. If you guys don't have groups like that, there's always Craigslist, there's always garage sales even man, just do what you got to do to find shoes for cheap. Because like I said, those local meetups, there's no fees. That's the best way. You don't need to wait for shipping for a shoe to come in. You can get it right there and then, and that's awesome.

We're going to have a whole another video about safe practises though from meetups because I know a lot of you guys, like I say, are younger readers and there's some sketchy stuff that can happen. So I just want you guys to be safe. So check that next video first before doing local meetups because yeah, I don't want you guys getting into trouble or things like that. Okay?

So the last thing, if you don't use any of those avenues, obviously you can try to cop for retail. Copping for retail is going to be the best investment you can make, however it's really, really difficult. On drop day, your local Foot Locker and stuff has shoes that you know are going to be rare, like Jordan 1 Bred, there's going to be a line, you're going to have to do a little bit of camping out, you're going to have to raffle, you're going to have to do what it takes. Even if you miss out That's okay because you're trying to create opportunity and by being there in that line you're creating community, you're finding out what other people are buying, what other people are selling. Make friends. So that's another way.

The other way would be to do the online releases like Yeezy release days, Jordan SNKRS app release days. Really be on top of your game and find as many avenues as you can to create inventory for yourself. Like I said, you don't need to have a beater box with 10 plus shoes to get to selling. If you can get one Yeezy, that's the same flip value almost as an entire beater box of shoes. That 200, 300, $400 profit line, that's very, very in-line with what would happen if you sold an entire beater box. From one Yeezy. So yeah, the beater boxes look cool, but honestly, if you can cop Yeezy's for retail, that's the best way to go.

Make sure you just build up your inventory. Don't build up inventory on bad shoes though. Okay? You have to be smart. If you go to your local Foot Locker and you see things sitting on shelves, it's been there for one, two, three, four days, that's a good sign there's no market for that shoe, so don't buy it. If nobody's buying it for retail at Foot Locker, nobody's going to buy it for flipped resell value on GOAT app. That's just how it is. So you have to be really smart. You have to see where the hype is. You have to see how limited these stocks are. If they're doing raffles for it, that's a good sign that there's going to be a flip value. Just be smart. Do your research, like I said. It's always learning. It's always adapting. Try your best to build up your inventory.

SNEAKER HUSTLE

5. HOW TO PRICE

How to correctly price used or new. There's not a set formula for a correct and incorrect way to do this but there are a lot of good guidelines that I can give you guys to show you how I price my shoes and price them to move pretty quickly. Let's get right into it.

Let's start off with the new shoes because new shoes are easy, it's very clean cut. There's no changes in new shoes, you'll either have it new or it's not new so a new shoe, like I said, is dead stock. That means it hasn't been worn, hasn't been tried on for the most part, no creases, nothing weird, it's 100% new. That pricing, for the most part, will always remain the same.

You can find that price or the market price on StockX, GOAT, eBay, and that price will pretty much be the same wherever you look. If a shoe is selling for ... This cream is $450, I think, right now new. If it's selling for about $450 on StockX, you can expect that that's where the market will be contingent everywhere so it won't vary too much. You might see some where people will price it maybe 15, $20 lower so they can make it sell quicker but, for the most part, if you look in the median, so whatever the highest number is selling for and the lowest number, you kind of just find the middle ground.

There might be some that sell for $500, there might be some that sell for $400, but a median will be $450 and that's the ground you want to look at. That's what I mean by competitive market pricing, you're not pricing it too high, you're not pricing it too low, you're pricing it exactly where people will buy. People will buy, trust me, it's pretty set in stone. If you guys have a Yeezy, for the most part, it will sell. Most DS shoes have bidding numbers already on there so you guys will move those.

Concept that we're going to be going over right here though, used sneakers, there is no formula on how to price used sneakers correctly, there's not anything. It's not like you can say, "Okay, so there's one scratch on this shoe," every scratch is minus $5 from the total or it's missing the box and now that's an automatic minus $50. There's nothing like that. Every used shoe is different and every shoe has a specific pricing so you really, really, really have to watch what the market is on used shoes because people will come at you.

They come at me all the time. They say, "Oh, you're pricing your used shoes crazy high." Again, that's not me pricing it, that's what the market is pricing it at. The best way to find used shoe prices is to look at GOAT app. I know I say it all the time but I really use this resource for everything I do. I'm not sponsored by them but it really is the most efficient way to find prices for used shoes.

StockX doesn't let you sell used shoes so that's where we can't look at all. eBay, it's a little bit harder because the pricing will change all the time on there, there's not really any middle ground. GOAT, you can find it really easy. If you look over here, what you do is you go look onto the shoe, you click on the price, the size, condition that you have, and then if you scroll down it says recently sold.

Recently sold, you can see the dates of prices that these shoes have sold for actually in that same condition. If you put it in as used, it's going to show you used prices that it sold for, not new prices. That's really nice because that way you can find the middle number between those six and you have a good middle ground. That's only step one of how I price used shoes.

Step two is you have to not only look at the prices it sold for but you have to look at the prices that they're selling for right now. You click on that sneaker, you click on used shoes that are selling right now in the same size, and you look at what other people are pricing their shoes for. Like I said, it's going to be different every single time. Some of them will have markings, some will have no box, some will have bad creases, some will be missing the insoles, you really have to check what prices your exact condition are going for.

For instance, let's say we're looking for a V2 Cream with no box. We're not even going to look at the ones with boxes and we're just going to look only for the ones without boxes. You just want to click on those, click on those, look at the prices they're selling for. For the most part, I would say that if it's in pretty good condition, even if there's no box, you could sell a Yeezy Cream for about 380-ish at the used price and that's a good median.

That's the two-fold method that I use to price used shoes. Again, it's not exactly set every single time, there will be variations. The thing is, is that you can have priced a shoe today for $500 and that shoe literally tomorrow could be worth $600, $700, $800 or it could be on the opposite end of that spectrum and be worth 100 bucks. You really don't know because the market is continually in flux, especially for used shoes.

You'll always see that the limited edition shoes will sell for higher values than non-limited edition so a good rule of thumb is to never set GRs for higher than the selling retail rate. I say that because you can't flip a GR if they're still sitting on shelves, you just can't do it. They will have those on shelves so there's no demand for it. Remember what I said about supply and demand, if there is a high demand there won't be any on the shelves. If there's a low demand, there'll be a lot on the shelves.

That means you can't sell those shoes online for more money because you can still go into Foot Locker right now and pick up that pair for retail pricing. You really need to look closely at the market and make sure you're only buying shoes at are collaborations, are limited runs or that you just can tell there's a lot of hype and you know it'll sell out fast and that way there will be room to flip.

Obviously, for the Yeezy it's super easy, you know every Yeezy is going to flip, for the most part, if it's a 350 or a 750. The 700 Wave Runner, I don't think that's going to have any flip value, to be honest. It looks terrible, just like how the Calabasas and the Yeezy Cleats were. You got to really tailor your expectations to what you've seen the market going. If people are saying those are really ugly, you can be certain that nobody's going to be buying those for more than retail.

Another important thing you want to do when you're pricing your shoes is to take into account taxes, fees, and shipping costs you will have to use to send those shoes out, I know I hear it all the time. You're selling these shoes for these prices but is that including taxes and fees or how does that work? For the most part, I don't look at the number I'm setting it at, I look at the number I'm going to make. That includes the 9.5% fee or whatever on GOAT, plus the $5 transaction. You also have to take in consideration that 2.9% fee through PayPal.

It's a lot of taxes and fees and stuff but, honestly, even after all of that is said and done, you will still make about the same money or maybe even a little bit more than what you could sell it for locally because the local pricing will obviously be the lowest you can find because you don't need to worry about those fees and taxes and stuff. Thankfully on GOAT, seriously, you can sell shoes for a lot higher on there, and people will buy them, than if you sold it locally.

Make sure you look at those fees and those prices and stuff and pay attention to the small number, not to the big number. Your take away won't be that $450, your take away will be that $410, $405 or whatever it is. Make sure you guys take that into account when you guys are pricing your shoes or else you'll lose out on a couple extra bucks here and there.

What I do want to mention is that, if you're going to try to sell your shoes, I always try to put it for the lowest possible bid on there. It will have some variations for Yeezies and stuff. Say for Yeezy Creams or Yeezy Turtle Doves and things like that, there will be a lot of used shoes for there so there's a lot of competition for what you're trying to sell for. The best way to make that sale is to put it at the lowest pricing. You have to really make sure you have an idea of how much profit you want to make when you're pricing your shoes.

For Yeezies, obviously they will sell no matter what so you can be a little bit stingier on your pricing. Don't go for the lowest price, sell it for a little bit more, sell it for higher than the median, that way you can make more value over time. If it's a shoe that is going to be a lot harder to move like a Nike SB, those don't really sell very quickly so you really want to make sure you're pricing yours at the lowest possible value.

Another key tip for when you're pricing your shoes is that if a shoe doesn't sell within maybe two or three weeks I would lower the value on it. That way you can get more interest, people will really see, "Oh, this shoe is less than a hundred bucks, I should probably take a look at it, maybe I can flip it." That's going to be the mindset a lot of people have when they're trying to sell or buy shoes. Make sure you just keep lowering your prices, not too much but lowering it just a bit so that it gets the attention of buyers.

Another very important point that can't be taken for granted, is that you need to start off your highest price higher than what you actually want. This goes more for when you're selling locally than it is ... I guess it goes for eBay and GOAT too but, for the most part, it works for a local sale. You never start your bid exactly what you want it at. Okay, say I want $400 for this, I want $400. I'm not going to put on the pricing that I want $400. Reason being is that maybe there's somebody willing to spend $420, $430, $450 for this shoe. I'm going to put it not too high because people will be like this guy's trying to rip people off.

Nothing over $500 but I'm going to put this shoe for $450, and that way you put OBO, or best offer, and people will offer up. If somebody gives you something like, say, $430, that's $30 higher than what you would've wanted in your price so you take that bid. Doesn't necessarily mean whatever you're putting out there you're going to get, but at least that higher number will give you more wiggle room of how much you can actually sell it for.

If you sold this for $400 exactly, there's going to be a buyer really quick so in terms of trying to make the most profit you can you really have to market it correctly. Make sure you always start very high, you're going to have a whole bunch of low ballers and that's okay. Low ballers will happen no matter what, GOAT app, eBay, StockX, local, it's going to happen. People will always try to find a steal even when the price is already low so that's why you keep your price higher than what you want, not too much higher. If you really want it to move, then put it exactly the number you want.

Again, this isn't an exact science, guys, but that is the formula on how I price my shoe. If I can't find a shoe on GOAT for seeing the used prices and stuff, then I'll go to eBay, check those prices on the sold listing so very important. On eBay, you can pretty much list anything you want on there for any price, that doesn't necessarily mean that's what it's selling for. If you go on that sidebar on eBay, there's a sold listings. You click on that, it shows you exactly how much shoes have sold for in that same condition.

Yeah, pricing is critical, guys. If you price your shoe wrong, people will not even take a look at it. If I see a Yeezy for way higher than what I know the market price is, I'm just going to keep looking, keep scrolling, not even paying attention to their shoe, and that thing is going to sit. If you do not price correctly, you can be in a hole and have a whole bunch of shoes that you can't move so just make sure you price it correctly the first time, follow these tips, and you'll be A okay.

SNEAKER HUSTLE

6. SHIPPING AND OTHER COSTS

How do you cut costs and where do you buy your materials to ship, and just how do you save money overall, because selling shoes can get expensive. Not only do you need to worry about shipping costs, you need to worry about shipping material, so that's like boxes, tape, things like that. And you also need to worry about fees.

Anyway, let's get right into it. So first things first, what I wanted to talk about is what method do I use to ship my shoes? So there's obviously three main sources if you guys would live in the US which is; USPS, FedEx and UPS. In the UK its Royal Mail Signed For or a courier - I find Hermes to be quite inexpensive.

So depending on what I'm shipping, if it's from my web store, I typically use United States Postal Service. The reason being is because they have the cheapest prices, and the price that I use to ship the shoes, if it's an individual shoe from Hawaii, it usually costs about $20 which is kind of a lot, but it's what you have to do.

If you're selling between a person to person, like say you're going to have a PayPal transaction, a. PayPal invoice, you need to make sure that shipping is a priority for you. If it takes too long to get there, people will not want to do business with you again.

If the box is damaged before it gets there, people don't want to do business with you again. So make sure you shell out that little bit of extra money so that you can get a good quality product to your customer. I use USPS, I know UPS can charge a little bit more, but that's preference-based, I guess. And FedEx, I don't even use FedEx at all, so I'm not too sure about the cost there. But just from what I've been researching, if you can fit a shoe into one of those large flat rate boxes, which I really don't think you can unless they're like kid shoes, then USPS is the way to go.

Okay, and with that being said, the size of your box matters when you ship something out because USPS or UPS or FedEx will all charge you based off of the dimensions of your box. So I've actually found the optimal dimension of a box that I used to ship out shoes and these usually fit shoes that go up to size 13 or 14. Yeah, it's just the optimum price and bang for your buck. I'm putting a link to the boxes I use which might be helpful. The reason why I choose this box is because, like I said, if it's a shoe perfectly.

There may be a little bit of packing involved, so I use packing paper or whatever it is. I really just use whatever's around the house. You guys can use things like this, seriously, your brown paper bags from your shopping, grocery shopping, and things like that, you could use that to pack material. And for the most part that gets the job done, you save money there. This box set, I believe through Amazon, is for 75 boxes and that seems like a lot, but it actually makes it for like one dollar per box, which is a really, really good, in my opinion.

I've seen people comment saying you should use the eBay boxes because they're cheaper. Unfortunately, if you're going to send to GOAT or you're going to send to a client, it doesn't really look good for your business if you're using an eBay box because it doesn't express YOU. So I try to use these plain brown boxes, and like I said, this one's from Amazon and it cost $75 for 75 boxes. This is perfect size box. You cut costs there. If you buy an individual box from a store like Walmart or something like that, it'll be pretty pricey.

I believe I was using Target before, and Target, for one of their boxes, it was like four ... three or $4 and that was way, way, way too much. You're going to lose out on a lot of profit that way. So the best way to do that is to buy in bulk because if you buy in bulk, you obviously get better pricing. And trust me, if you guys are really going to get into reselling, you'll use all 75 of those boxes. I'm on my second set already and I need to order again. So I would highly suggest checking out that link at the end of this chapter, clicking on it and you'll get the best bang for your buck there.

So another cost that could add up for you guys is not only the box you use, but also the tape that you guys use. Tape I found is way more expensive than boxes and it's crazy. So this is the tape that I use. It's this Duck brand, HD Clear, whatever it is. But, again, buying in bulk makes for cheaper products. So I think this one was 20-something bucks or something like that, for six rolls. And you got to also look at the length of how much you're getting, not how much of these individual things you're buying. The length is what matters. Okay? It doesn't matter if you get eight of these and you only get like 400 yards or metres. The length is what matters because that's how much you can use.

So that's an important tip. Again, this'll be at the end of the chapter via Amazon, 20-something dollars. Really good deal. Like I said, you'll use this all the time when you're shipping. So great investment there.

In terms of shipping and packaging, that's pretty much it that I use. Like I said, I try to recycle things that I can. Another good tip, if you guys do not have that much money to buy $75 worth of boxes or $20 worth of tape, is to reuse the material that you get from your purchases. So if you buy something from GOAT, you buy something from Nike Adidas.com, it does come in a box already so what you do is you just take off all of that tape and postage stuff on there. You cross out all of the numbers and things like that and reuse the box.

You're going to have to get some of your own tape, but I'm sure there's a couple pieces of duct tape or something lying around your house. So utilise what you can. Like I said, try to recycle as much as you can because if you can use that box that saves you that extra dollar from not touching your 75 boxes. And I mean, it does add up guys. This is if you're dealing with a lot, a lot of shoes. Start off with what you have. Like I've said before, instead of buying product, you can even sell your old used shoes, things like that. So really start off small and then when you start to get more product and you're trying to sell a lot more, that's when you can buy those bulk items. And trust me, it saves a lot of money; boxes and shipping and tape and all of that stuff can add up. So that's my best advice there.

Also, what I want you guys to focus on in terms of like fees and pricing and things like that, you really need to make sure that you're maximising every single possibility you can to make a sale and to make profit. So that also means you have to look at fees. So I know the eBay fee is like nine-something percent. The StockX fee is somewhere in that same ballpark and honestly the GOAT fee is in that same ballpark as well. People will say that GOAT is more expensive, but honestly it's so arbitrary for those little fees, and that difference, that I'd rather pay slightly more in terms of like a couple bucks to deal with a better customer service product, like GOAT, than using StockX and dealing with their very bad customer service.

Because if something goes wrong, it really is just more trouble for you. Same thing with eBay. I know there's a lot of charge backs and problems through that venue, so just be careful. You'll see that those variations can add up, but if you price your shoes according to what you want as your final valuation, and not the sale price itself, then you're in the clear anyway. So what does that mean? If I'm selling a shoe for $500 on GOAT, that means I'm expecting to make 445 back, so I'm only looking at the 445 number. And if that 500 is reasonable to sell, then that's good because I can make that 445 definitively. Focus on that, that way you can save money as well.

But just be wary. I mean, be wary of the fees it will catch up to you as well. There's a fee on GOAT, I think a 2.9% fee for PayPal, and it seems like it's a small number as well, but it can add up. I've actually just cashed out on like, I think a $3,000 ... $3,000 I cashed out and with that 2.9% fee it was something like 80 bucks, or something like that. So it does add up. But I mean, again, that's only if you're dealing with large volumes of money. In the long run, if you can make a sale through GOAT, it really doesn't matter too much. Ultimately the best way you'll save on all of those costs though, is to sell locally.

Selling locally you don't need to ship, you don't need to pack, you don't need to deal with any of that. It's literally just a face-to-face transaction, cash for shoes, and that is the best way that you can go about doing that. So that is why I try to sell all of my shoes locally before I start looking outside to sell via shipping and things like that. So, again, maximise your profit revenue and that will be through selling locally. That's why I say it's so important to create connections with people in the community, because if you don't, you lose out on that opportunity to sell locally and you lose out on all that potential revenue.

So make sure when you do these sales and whatnot, you make it ... You're actually a business, present yourself as a business. Make sure you're professional when you're writing to people via Message and stuff like that. Make sure you use politeness. It's just really basic things that people forget all the time. But if you really want to maximise profit, you need to do these things. So with that, the next chapter will actually be about focusing on how to do a local sale. I don't want a lot of you younger kids to go out there making sales locally, because there's a lot of sketchy stuff that can go on. So the next episode I'm going to talk about product safety or just being safe when you're selling shoes.

Shipping Boxes ▶ http://amzn.to/2fmp1qF
Duct Tape ▶ http://amzn.to/2eImIho

SNEAKER HUSTLE

7. CAUTIONARY TALES

Selling shoes online for the most part is some of the sketchiest dealings you could ever be doing. It's sketchy. There's a lot of fakes out there. There's a lot of people that will try to steal money from you. There's just a lot of crazy, crazy things that can get you into a lot of trouble, and you end up losing money, more so than you're making money. That's a scary thought.

A lot of it is that I know a lot of you guys are watching that are very, very young. By very young, I mean like you're 12, 13, 14, 15 years old. I just want you guys to know that in the sneaker community, there's a lot of good guys out there, but there are also a lot of bad guys. By bad guys, I mean there's people that want to try to take your money or scam you and things like that. Just try to follow these like guidelines and you should be okay.

One of the first things that you should know is that if you can get a third party person like eBay, Goat or StockX to help you with your sales, that is probably the number one thing that will save you a lot of time and hassle with fakes and chargebacks and scams, okay? The reason why a third party is good is because you're protected. You're protected from those charge backs. You're protected from getting fake items and things of that nature.

Let's go over it, I guess one by one. eBay is probably the most sketchy out of those three in terms of reselling, just because there are a lot of fakes on there. eBay cannot monitor every single item that is posted onto their forums. That is where the problem lies. You'll see a lot of fakes. You're going to have to legit check for yourself in pictures, if you're buying.

If you're selling, you're going to have a lot of people that are trying to swindle you. One of the main things on eBay is you should only sell to people that have higher than zero ratings. Zero ratings are basically, I'm going to assume false accounts that people use in order to create chargebacks, get free shoes and never pay you for it. Just be careful of that. There's a lot of people with zero ratings. If you see a zero rating for the most part, it probably is something is up, especially if they're trying to message you on the side and say, "okay, let's avoid eBay. Let's just go straight to PayPal. I'll send you cash this way. We can do it that way, so you'll save from the fees." Don't buy into that. Pay the extra fees, so you have seller protection. Just pay.

You want to do your transaction within eBay. Don't create PayPal invoices. Don't do it. There are a lot of ways that they can scam you, and you'll never see your shoes or your money ever again. Just avoid that -- stick with selling in eBay.

For Goat and StockX, it's really easy, because you're never going to interact with your buyer. That makes it really nice. As a seller, you know that you're going to get your money in and out. It's quick and efficient. That's why I like selling on Goat honestly. They're a great third party. You send it right to them. They send it out to your buyer and that's it. As soon as it gets to their factory, you're getting paid. That's quick and easy. Avoids a lot of hassles. Avoids a lot of scams. It just is a very safe method to use.

Beyond that, I was touching earlier about PayPal. PayPal can be a really useful resource if you're trying to buy and sell via like Facebook forums. The reason why is because local sales, you avoid a lot of fees. You avoid a lot of ... Just, you can save more money. You don't need to ship. It's a lot less hassle if you know what you're doing. What does that mean? Is that you can sometimes still have to ship, which is okay, especially if you're living in Hawaii, like inter Island transactions are possible, but I feel like they're only possible if you use PayPal to invoice.

PayPal invoice, it creates that third party thing that I was saying again. The reason why is because you have seller protection. You create an invoice. If you send them your product and they try to get chargeback money or they don't pay you or things like that, it lessens the damage that can be dealt. You're going to get paid automatically, because it's an invoice. He's going to have to pay to that invoice. It creates a receipt. A receipt is good for not only the seller but the buyer as well. If you can do that, that is a really the safest way.

Some people will say, "Okay, can we do friends and family?" You can change money that way, but you don't get seller protection and that's a hassle, because if they chargeback that money for their account, you're out of a shoe and there's nobody you can go complain to for your money back. Whereas if you have the invoice, and they try to do chargebacks and things like that, you're more protected because you have a piece of paper saying, "Okay, they acknowledge that you sent the item to them." That is a big thing. You guys want to be protected online. There's a lot of scams, like I said, a lot of fakes that can be sold. You just want to make sure that you're in the best possible scenario to send out shoes to people and create money and get it back on your own.

From personal experience, I've actually had problems with chargebacks and things like that. People say, "I'm not getting the right shoe or the shoe you sent me as fake." Honestly that is some of the most BS you can ever hear. All of the shoes that I get are from Sole Supremacy. For the most part, I know every single one is legit. There's no way that they're fake shoes. People will say they're fake though. This is why, because if you're selling a used shoe, there's no way, if they ask for a return, you can know that the exact same condition of the shoe you sent is the same shoe you'll be receiving back, which is why there's no returns on any of my shoes that I sell, because it's used, it's impossible to tell.

Whereas a new shoe, okay, if it's in new condition, they didn't try it on. Okay, that makes sense. Here's the thing, because if there's no third party, like transaction and stuff like that, like sending it to Goat where they authenticate first, if you sell your shoe to somebody, like say in Chicago, I sent it out to Chicago, the guy gets it, he sees that it's real. What is he going to do though if he's sketchy and wants to scam me? He puts a fake shoe out, exact same shoe. I send him a bred easy. Then he puts in a fake bread easy and says, "Okay, this is a fake." Because the exact same size and same model and everything, and he's going to send it back as a fake when you actually you sent him the real shoe. That's why it's important to get all of your paperwork and documentation, important to take pictures of stuff that you send out and just be as well documented as you can, because things like that happen. There's a lot of sketchy people in the world, guys. There's a lot of sketchy sneaker heads. It's very unfortunate because cause just shoes, but people see it as a very lucrative thing and the best way to avoid all of this stuff is to stay protected and use these tips.

If people are trying to do sneaker trades as well online, I for the most part will always avoid that. In general, I'm not a big fan of sneaker trades. It's never an even transaction because values are perceived differently, especially on used shoes. It's really, really hard to find a perfect medium where it's a fair trade. Usually somebody is getting a little bit less or a lot more honestly than the other guy. It's crazy. Especially trying to send a shoe from here to somebody in Chicago. They have the to send a shoe back to me, there's so many things that can go wrong with that. I really, really, really am suggesting do not try to do sneaker trades over shipping and things like that. There's a lot of things that can go wrong. It's just not worth it.

If you can do a local deal, like local sneaker trades, that's okay. I know there's going to be a lot of guys that say "Well, I do sneaker trades all the time through shipping. We email and just back and forth. It's safe." Yeah, there's going to be times when it's safe. For all those times it's safe, there's going to be like three or four times more fraud possibilities. I know, like I said, most of you guys are younger, so you can't really sniff out those frauds, and it's terrible. Just avoid it all together and you'll be fine.

If people try to hit you up on your Instagram to buy shoes and it's like, okay, I'm going to DM you real quick, here's my number, whatever, call this and do this and do that. If they're trying to get straight up money for you or it seems sketchy or something seems off, use your better judgement and realise that it's not a good idea. There will be other opportunities to sell your shoe. You do not need to force it and sell to somebody that seems sketchy or off. Same thing with any deals. If you try to buy something online, if it seems too good to be true, it's probably a fake or something is definitely wrong with that shoe, okay? If you see it COS4 for $400, that is not a real COS 4. Let's be real. It's just that's how it is. You have to use some common sense, common sneaker sense, common sneaker head sense. I don't even know if sneaker heads have common sense. I mean it's we spend all of this money on these things that like, I don't know. I don't know.

I know it seems like some standard information, but I know at the same time there's a lot of you guys that have not run into these problems. I think it's critically important that you guys get it out of the way early to avoid all of these scams and frauds and things like that.

SNEAKER HUSTLE

8. HOW ABOUT INSTAGRAM?

Now, one of the biggest questions was people want to know how to make it big as an Instagram seller, so selling sneakers on Instagram. You know, I'm not a big fan of selling on Instagram, so in this video, I'm going to be telling you guys the top three reasons why I choose not to sell sneakers on Instagram and why I think it's just a bad idea overall.

Number one is that it's really tough to build an audience on Instagram. The reason why it's kind of simple. There's so much sneaker authentication apps and stuff now that you guys can choose from and stuff and you know that what you're getting is supposed to be legit and authentic. I say supposed to, because there have been mishaps with some certain sneaker apps where you're not really getting authentic shoes. However, for the most part, those apps have bridged the gap where people can buy from them safely and the prices are relatively affordable. It's not you're buying from an expensive consignment store and stuff. Because of that, it allowed a lot of people to move over to that platform, and that means that there's going to be less people wanting to buy from you on Instagram.

Like, what do you have to offer that's different and what do you have to offer that's different than what they could get on like Goat App? I know typically the biggest answer here would be, "I have a better price. If you guys buy through my site, then I don't need to worry about fees and stuff so I can sell things for cheaper." Yes, that's one thing that would make sense for selling on Instagram. But the problem is that if you have a hundred followers on there, how are you going to get exposure and how are people going to hear about your product? You could have a really good sneaker story. You know, you can be selling a lot of shoes on Instagram and stuff, but if no one knows about you, it is very difficult to move shoes. And for the vast majority people that don't have a huge platform like on YouTube and stuff, it can be very hard to sell on Instagram, because that building that audience takes time and some people just don't have the time to put into it.

There's some OGs in the game that sell on Instagram, and they have tens of thousands of followers, and whatnot and they sell shoes really quick, but it's because they're well known in the game. So if you guys do want to build an Instagram, you just have to give consistent service, consistent deals and stuff, and then hopefully people will find you by word of mouth. But for the most part, it is very, very difficult to find an audience on there. Why would you choose to sell to your hundred followers on your Instagram, whereas you have hundreds of thousands of people on Goat App looking at shoes all the time. My thing is that it's better to make the quick sale than it is to make a bigger profit margin because in this game, volume is everything, so that's why I choose to sell them on the apps and why I don't sell on Instagram and stuff. It's tough and I just wouldn't recommend it if you guys are just getting started.

For number two, I've got to let you guys know that as well

as not selling shoes on Instagram, I also do not buy any shoes on Instagram. The reason why is because scammers are everywhere. On Instagram, you get scammed all the freaking time for sneakers. That's why there's a bad stigma for people that I try to buy on Instagram because it's like, "How do I know these things are legit? How do I know you're legit?" Like, you've never done business before, you see this account selling Yeezys for maybe 200 bucks for retail and you're like, Whoa, that's not a bad deal. Maybe it's a little bit dirty or something. This guy could be legit." However, you'd have no idea, man. Until that transaction is made, you have no basis to go evaluate.

Another problem here is that they'll tell you, "Okay, I can give you this price, but you got to pay through PayPal friends and family so I don't need to worry about fees and stuff." Then maybe it's a legit shoe. Maybe he's legit, he sends you the shoe, but it's in a different condition than you saw on his Instagram. Or it ends up being unauthentic altogether, which would be the worst case scenario, and you're asking yourself now, " I don't understand. This guy has 100,000 followers and stuff on Instagram so he should have been legit. Right?"

The problem with that is that you can have a 100,000 followers on Instagram and it may be costs you 500 bucks to get to that point, because a lot of people in that sneaker Instagram selling thing, they understand that you can buy followers on Instagram, and that creates this bad perception where you don't really know what's the true following for this person. Are any of these guys even real?

My biggest thing with that is don't get swept up and seeing a huge follower count and then believing, "Nah, this guy has to be legit. I can buy from him on Instagram. It's fine. I can send PayPal friends and family. Like, I'm not going to get scammed." First of all, you should never use PayPal friends and family. That is ridiculous. Always go through goods and service so at least you have some kind of protection. Friends and family, you can't get protected on that, so it's not a good idea to ever. Pay the fee, whatever. Pay that a little bit higher priced so you can have the protection just in case.

Secondly, if you guys think that this site is reputable, don't look at the follower count like I was saying. Instead, look at the likes on their post. Now, if I see an account that has 100,000 followers on it, right, and he's getting maybe 50 likes on each of his pictures on average? That's a pretty big discrepancy, guy's. Like, That's a huge discrepancy. Why would somebody that has 100,000 followers only be getting 50 likes on the picture? Because that percentage is .001 or something. It's very unlikely that those are actual followers because nobody's liking his stuff.

Now, if you see maybe 2000 likes or 3000 likes or something on a 100,000 followers, that's a more manageable number, like maybe 3% of his following. Okay? That would be a little bit more inclined. But again, I would check different pictures and stuff because you're also able to buy likes on certain pictures. People will try to manipulate you on Instagram. So just be aware, man. That's why I usually just buy it through a sneaker authentication app because then at least I know it's going to be legit for the most part, and if it's not, then I can get a refund and it won't be a hassle because that's an actual reputable business.

Now, number three why I don't sell on Instagram is because it is way faster to sell on sneaker apps these days, man. I know a lot of people will hate on this because they're saying, "Well, it kind of ruined the profit margins that you can get for sneakers," but I can rebuttal that by saying Jordan 1 prices have never been higher ever in the history of the world right now, and that is because of sneaker apps, man.

It takes no time at all to get this going off the ground, man. Because for an app like Goat, you don't see the face of the person behind whoever's selling the shoe.

Everything is anonymous. You can't even message that guy for the shoe, so deals go quick and you protected by Goat App. That's important, man, because when you think about it, anonymity in the sneaker game is huge. Then you don't need to show that you're reputable, because Goat App is the one that's reputable. You can have zero followers and sell a shoe for $1,500. That is incredible, and you can't do that on Instagram. You would need a strong following. You would need a strong reputation. You'd need to be doing this for a number of years in order to make a sale of that kind of volume. There's no questions asked when you sell through sneakers app, no BS, no chargebacks, no issues like that. It's just straight up selling sneakers for profit. Again, I don't mind paying a small fee for the fact that I have all this protection and that I'm reaching an audience of a lot of people. It saves a lot of time and it lets you earn money faster.

That is my three things on why I don't utilise Instagram. I hope you guys take that information. However, if some of you guys are doing well with your sneaker resale business through Instagram, that's all well and good, man. But for the guys that are just starting off and for the beginners, that's why I believe that is not a good idea to sell on Instagram and instead it's better to go through the app system. That is my take on that.

SNEAKER HUSTLE

9. OUTRO

What more can I say? There is so much information out there for you to educate yourself. Safe some money. Start Small and hustle hustle hustle. You may even cop some shoes for free.

Check out the free FREE Sneaker Video Resources. Sign up here.

https://www.sneakercollecting.website/signup

ABOUT THE AUTHOR

Leonard Payne is nowhere near young and certainly not a millennial. He's an old boomer and lives near to the Peak District in England. He is retired and supplements his meagre pension by publishing books. If you need to contact him try rev.leonard.payne@protonmail.com

www.ingramcontent.com/pod-product-compliance
Lightning Source LLC
Chambersburg PA
CBHW030953240526
45463CB00016B/2532